Continental Queens

By Kristine Cobb

Illustrated By Chloe Coulibaly

Copyright © 2024 PREMIUM BOOK PUBLISHERS

All rights reserved. No part of this book may be used, reproduced, scanned, or distributed in any printed or electronic form by no means whatsoever without written permission. Please do not copyright materials in violation of the author's right. Purchase only authorized editions. For more information, e mail all inquiries to info@Premiumbookpublishers.com. Published by Premium Book Publishers.

www.premiumbookpublishers.com

Printed in United States of America

Table of Contents

Dedication 1

North Carolina: 2

Hawaii: 4

Germany: 6

France: 8

Italy: 10

Brazil: 12

India: 14

Panama: 16

Philippines: 18

Kenya: 20

Sweden: 22

Dedication

This book is dedicated to my seven grandchildren Talisa, Zayden, Aaliyah, Ethan, Brayden, Avery and Vera ♥

North Carolina:

In America, there are many names for grandmother, but in Asheville, North Carolina, one of the common names for grandmother is "Granny."

Granny lives in Asheville, North Carolina. She loves to paint all kinds of pictures on her easel. Today, Granny is painting a picture of the Smoky Mountains that she can see from her backyard. Granny also likes to ride around in her new golf cart. Granny's grandkids also like to ride around with her in her golf cart. Granny drives her golf cart out on the back 40 she calls it. This is the 40 acres of trails that wind around beautiful pine trees and sparkling streams. Sometimes, Granny likes to go fishing with her grandkids, too. She likes teaching all her grandkids how to fish. One time, Granny caught a huge Bass fish, and her grandkids were so excited because when it was weighed, it weighed 12 pounds! Then Granny cleaned and scaled the fish and cooked it along with homemade French fries and coleslaw. Besides being lots of fun, Granny is an excellent cook and she's a darn good baker too!

Hawaii:

In Hawaii, the formal word for grandmother is "Kuku Wahine" or "Tutu Wahine."

However, "Tutu" is what most Hawaiians call their grandma.

Tutu is spending her Saturday selling her delicious fresh Hawaiian fruit on the beach. Tutu likes to visit with the other native island people and the tourists who go to the beach. She takes pride in the fruit she sells. Tutu is always in a good mood, especially on Saturdays at the beach. Tutu likes to tell the tourists how she has had the pleasure of eating these wonderful fruits like coconuts, pineapples, bananas, and mangos since she was a little girl. She tells them that her Tutu taught her at an early age how to plant these wonderful fruit trees and how to care for them. When Tutu goes back home from the beach she tends to all her fruit trees by making sure they get the proper amount of water and fertilizer. But Tutu doesn't have to worry too much because Hawaii is a paradise for growing delicious fruit because of its climate, warm temperatures, abundant rainfall, and fertile soil.

Germany:

The name for grandmother in Germany is "Oma"

Oma lives in Munich, Germany. Oma is busy this morning baking a cake for her grandson's birthday. The kitchen smells of sweet chocolate floating in the air. Today is her grandson Caleb's 15th birthday, and she just finished baking his favorite cake, "Black Forest" cake. Birthdays are special in Germany because this means that Caleb will not have to do any chores today. Oma is an excellent baker, and her family looks forward to celebrating and eating Oma's delicious cake. Oma learned how to bake when she was a teenage girl because her Oma taught her how to bake. Oma bakes all her desserts from scratch, and even her icing is homemade. Oma often bakes "streusel" on weekends for breakfast, especially when her grandchildren come to visit or spend the night. Oma has eight grandchildren, and they love to spend time at Oma's house. All of Oma's grandchildren want to learn to bake, so Oma is planning to teach them how to bake cake, cookies, pies, muffins, and streusel.

France:

In France, the French word for grandmother is "Grand'Mere", pronounced as (Grahn Mare)

Grand'Mere loves to shop for clothes. She prefers to shop in the small boutiques where she knows she will find unique, one-of-a-kind pieces of clothing to add to her already fabulous wardrobe. Grand'Mere has always loved to shop, and she is lucky to live in Paris, France where there are plenty of boutiques to shop in. Fashion is very important to Grand Mere. She has worked to maintain her slender figure so that her clothes will look flattering on her. Grand'Mere prides herself in always looking spectacular. She keeps her beautiful snowy white poodle-like hair done and always has her nails manicured and polished. Grand'Mere has two granddaughters who also love to go with Grand'Mere to shop for clothes and go to "Le Salon de manicure" to have their nails done as well. Grand'Mere truly has a passion for fashion!

Italy:

In Italy, the word for grandmother is Nona, pronounced with the long o sound

Nona is on her way back home from the market. Nona plans to cook her famous lasagna for her children and grandchildren this afternoon. Nona went to the market to buy fresh bread for her tasty garlic bread. She also bought fresh salad ingredients like romaine lettuce, onions, olives, and tomatoes. Nona is a wonderful cook because her Nona taught her how to cook fantastic dishes such as lasagna when she was a young teenager. Nona uses the same special ingredients that her Nona used to make all her delicious pasta and bread. Nona has a secret sourdough recipe that she uses to make her pasta and bread. Everyone in Nona's family can't wait to visit Nona, sit at the table, and indulge at dinnertime. Everything Nona cooks puts a smile on her family's faces. Nona also has a smile on her face because she enjoys cooking for her family, and today, Nona has special plans to teach her granddaughter how to cook lasagna.

Brazil:

In Brazil the name for grandmother is "Vova."

Vova's favorite activity is riding her bike. Vova loves to bike through the beautiful parks in Brasilia, Brazil. She particularly likes to ride around sunset. Today, she is riding to her friend's house to give her a beautiful bouquet of blue hydrangea flowers to help cheer her up. Vova grows these flowers in her garden that surrounds her "Pergolato"- (A pergolato is the outdoor kitchen area). Vova has a large family, and she has seven grandchildren. She is looking forward to this Sunday when she and her grandchildren will ride on the highway that is closed every Sunday just for people and families like Vova's to ride their bikes on without the concern of car traffic. When Vova and her family are finished with their bike ride they will go back to her house and eat dinner. Vova is also a wonderful cook. Therefore, everyone loves to eat at Vova's Pergolato (outdoor kitchen) where they all enjoy eating and listening to music along with dancing while being surrounded by Vova's exquisite flowers on all sides of the Pergolato.

India:

The name for grandmother in India is Nani

Nani is busy this morning baking Vadi. Nani's grandchildren love the taste of the pink and yellow desert. Today is a special holiday in India because Nani's family is celebrating "Diwali."

Diwali is the "Hindu festival of lights." Besides creating delicious deserts, Nani and her grandchildren are creating a Rangoli decoration to celebrate Diwali. So, today Nani and her grandchildren are going to create a beautiful Rangoli design using pink, green, orange, and dark red colored sand. They have also placed several lit round small candles within a circular pattern to decorate the tabletop at the entrance of Nani's home.

The Rangoli represents the happiness, positivity, and liveliness of a household. It is intended to welcome "Lakshmi" (the goddess of wealth and good luck)."

Panama:

In Panama, the word for grandmother is Abuela

Abuela sells her beautiful handmade pottery at the market in downtown Casco Viejo, Panama.

Many tourists flock to the downtown Casco Viejo market to buy handmade unique and artistic items. Today, Abuela is selling her beautiful pottery at the downtown market. Sometimes, Abuela sells her exquisite quilts, tablecloths, and napkins, which are embroidered with brightly colored hand-sewn floral designs. Abuela loves to sew and her cheerful quilts, tablecloths, and napkins are frequently purchased by the tourists at the market. Abuela also loves to create and design pottery that she makes by using the clay from the earth in her own backyard. Abuela is happy and proud to share some of her Panamanian culture by creating her handmade items for local tourists to purchase.

Philippines:

"Lola" is the Filipino word for grandmother

Lola is practicing singing her songs for family Karaoke night tonight. Lola lives in Manilla, Philippines. Lola has always loved to sing, and she prides herself on being a very gifted singer. It is no doubt that Lola is an extremely gifted singer with her enormous voice range and sweet and smooth as butter sounding voice. Tonight, at Lola's house her children and grandchildren will join Lola to take turns singing all their favorite songs after they eat dinner. You see, Lola is also an excellent cook. Tonight, Lola is cooking two of her family's favorite dishes: vegetable stew and chicken adobo. Also, for dessert, Lola baked Flan and coconut cake. Even though tonight isn't a holiday or a birthday, it always feels special and exciting just to be in Lola's home with her. Lola is also well-liked by her neighbors because sometimes she gives them some of her delicious flan and coconut cake, and they also enjoy listening to Lola sing with her magnificent voice!

Kenya:

The name for grandmother in Kenya, Africa, is "Bibi."

Bibi lives in Nairobi, Kenya, in Africa. Bibi just finished pouring her morning Chai tea and is excited to begin beading one of her handmade "kanga gowns" that she just finished sewing. Bibi also makes colorful, exquisite, beaded jewelry in many different designs and patterns. Bibi's hard work and creativity have paid off well for Bibi as she is considered one of the wealthiest grandmothers in Kenya.

When Bibi was a young woman, she was a fashion model, and she always had an eye for the latest fashion. Bibi learned how to sew at a young age, and from the age of fourteen, Bibi knew that she wanted to be a fashion designer. Bibi's eldest granddaughter is learning how to sew and helps Bibi make her clothing and design the most colorful creations with elaborate beads for the celebrations of the Kenyan women.

After all, Bibi's granddaughter wants to be a fashion model and fashion designer, just like Bibi.

Sweden:

The name for grandmother in Sweden is Mormor

Mormor lives in Stockholm, Sweden. Mormor is baking cookies this morning.

She is excited because any minute now her whole family will be coming over to her house to bake cookies. Mormor and her family celebrate "The Twelve Days of Christmas" by doing twelve different activities. This year, the "first day of Christmas" is spent at Mormor's house baking many different kinds of cookies like sugar cookie cutouts of Christmas designs and gingerbread boys and girls. Mormor's grandchildren especially love to decorate the faces and clothes on the gingerbread boys and girls.

When all the cookies are finished, Mormor will place the assorted cookies in tin containers and give them away as Christmas presents to her eldest aunts and uncles.

"The Twelve Days of Christmas" traditions are special to Mormor because spending time with her family while they participate in each daily activity brings her family closer together. Tomorrow, Mormor and her family will celebrate "The second day of Christmas" by going ice skating.

Milton Keynes UK
Ingram Content Group UK Ltd.
UKHW051901191124
451300UK00003BA/11

● Fun with Engl

Gaffes & Goofs

How to be clearly understood

Norman Barrett
Illustrated by Anthony Bellue

Chambers

Editor: John Grisewood

Illustrations: Anthony Bellue
(Kathy Jakeman Illustration)

CHAMBERS
An imprint of Larousse plc
Elsley House, 24-30 Great Titchfield Street,
London W1P 7AD

First published by Chambers 1995

2 4 6 8 10 9 7 5 3 1

Illustrations copyright © Larousse plc 1995
Text © Norman Barrett 1995

All rights reserved. No part of this publication may be reproduced, stored in a retrieval system or transmitted by any means, electronic, mechanical, photocopying or otherwise, without the prior permission of the publisher.

A CIP catalogue record for this book is available from the British Library.

ISBN 0 550 32511 5

Printed in Spain

Contents

1 Between you and me and the gatepost
   (*Wrong case*)   4

2 There's many a slip (*Double meaning*)   8

3 A mute point (*Confusables*)   10

4 I am a jam doughnut (*Mistranslations*)   14

5 Dropping bricks (*Gaffes*)   15

6 It'll be all wrong on the night (*Solecisms*)   18

7 If you can't beat 'em ... (*New words*)   23

8 Head-scratching time (*Ambiguity*)   24

9 Hi there! What's the time? (*Time confusion*)   26

Answers   27

WRONG CASE

1 Between you and me and the gatepost

'Between you and me and the gatepost' is a saying which means 'in confidence; between ourselves'. The saying is a helpful reminder of how to avoid a common 'blunder' in the English language. 'Between you and me' is correct; but 'between you and I' is a mistake. Why, you may well ask?

People make this common mistake maybe because they have been constantly nagged not to say things like 'Terry and me went out last night' or 'You and me are the only ones who like carrots'. In these sentences 'I' is correct not 'me'.

Names of the pronouns

Pronouns are used in place of a noun. They refer to a person or thing already mentioned. Personal pronouns indicate the speaker, the person or people spoken to, or the person or thing spoken about. Pronouns can be the subject or object of a sentence.

	subject	object
The speaker(s)	I we	me us
Person(s) spoken to	you	you
Person(s) or thing(s) spoken about	he she they	him her them

'Between you and me and the gatepost, Fred and I have decided to learn how to fly.'

You can generally tell whether to use 'me' or 'I' by using the word alone. For example you would not say 'Me went out'. Therefore you shouldn't say 'Terry and me went out'. Nor, if you speak Received (or Standard) English, would you say 'He gave it to I'. The same test goes for the other 'pronouns', as these words used in place of names are called. The sports commentator who said 'Give he and his team-mates a pat on the back', would never have said 'Give he a pat on the back'.

WRONG CASE

Now test yourself by choosing the right pronoun for each of these sentences (answers on page 27):

1 The prize was given jointly to he/him and his sister.
2 This is from my brother and I/me.
3 My mother and I/me enjoy a game of Scrabble.
4 The argument is between they/them and we/us.
5 Him/He and she/her are identical twins.
6 It was I/me who broke the cup.
7 Who's that at the door? It's me/I.
8 You and me/I make a good partnership.

Self sacrifice

This uncertainty about how to use pronouns correctly can cause some people to misuse 'self' words — myself, herself, himself and so on. An advertisement for a holiday started: 'My wife, two kids and myself took the return ferry ...'. It's unlikely that the person who wrote the advertisement would ever write 'Myself took the return ferry ...' He

Me Tarzan, You Jane!

WRONG CASE

or she would quite correctly write, 'I took the return ferry.'

It may be that, because some people are unsure whether to use 'I' or 'me', they use 'myself' instead. But this in itself can lead to grammatical mistakes. So, correctly speaking, you should not say 'He invited my sister and myself to his party,' but rather: 'He invited my sister and me to his party.'

This is because 'he' can only invite '**him**self', 'you' can only invite '**your**self' and 'I' can only invite '**my**self'.

A suitable case for treatment

Pronouns are the only words in English that have what is known in grammar as 'case'. 'I' and 'me' are different forms of the same word. They are used according to the part they play in the sentence. 'I' is a 'doing' word — 'I did this,' ' I went there', and so on. 'He,' 'she' and 'they' are also 'doing' pronouns. The other forms of these words are 'me', 'him', 'her', and 'them' — you could call them 'done to' words. They are used when the person concerned has something done to him or her — 'Fred followed me', 'The bus waited for them'. (See panel, page 4.)

Now try it out on yourself. Which are correct? (answers on page 27)

1 Put yourself in my place.
2 I'm going to choose the books myself.
3 They found themselves in an awkward situation.
4 No one has informed either myself or my parents.
5 She left it for Peter and myself.
6 Jack, the twins and myself were the only ones present.
7 How's yourself.
8 I built the house myself.
9 The kittens were presents for my brother and myself.
10 The teacher gave ourselves a lesson.

THEY FOUND THEMSELVES IN AN AWKWARD SITUATION —

WRONG CASE

Are these different forms of pronouns really necessary? In English, the short answer is that they are not. We use them because that is how our language developed. At one time English, like Latin and German, had many inflections or different 'word endings'. These were and are necessary because the order of words in a sentence does not necessarily tell the listener or reader who is doing what to whom.

> Here is an example of German word order.
>
> *Kannst du mir bitte das Wasser reichen?*
>
> Can you to me please the water pass?

You have only to consider the pronoun 'you' to realize that these different forms are not needed in English. This is because in modern English there is only one form of 'you'. You can say 'I like you,' or 'You like me'. It may be used for one person or for more than one person. Other forms such as 'thou' and 'ye' have virtually died out.

But 'me' and the other different forms are very much alive in our language. So we should be able to use them in what has become their accepted and correct way. Remember, though, that rules can change over time and that it can sound 'stuffy' to obey every one of them.

There is, for example, the 'rule' that you must always use 'I', 'he' and 'she' after the verb 'to be' ('am', 'is', 'are', 'was', 'were'). Thus you should say 'It wasn't I' or 'This is she'. But this sounds a stiff and unnatural way of speaking. And if somebody asked 'Who left the fridge open?' What would you say? It is perfectly acceptable to say 'It wasn't me'.

And if the phone rang and a voice asked, 'Is that Jane Smith?', would you answer: 'This is she'? Probably not — unless you want to sound as if you'd swallowed a grammar book. Can you suggest a more appropriate reply? (answer on page 27).

DOUBLE MEANING

2 There's many a slip

The advertisement said 'Crash courses for pilots'. Anyone answering it would know that they could expect a series of flying lessons over a short period. For that's what a crash course means — learning to do something in double-quick time. It's just possible to misread the ad as learning how to crash a plane!

Although the advertisement for 'crash courses' could have a double meaning, it is very unlikely that anyone would think that the second meaning was intended.

This is true of most statements that have a double meaning. But if you say something that is capable of being taken in another way — usually funny or rude — don't be surprised if people laugh.

The art of double-meaning — or to use the French expression *double entendre* (which incidentally the French have never heard of) — is practised by comedians and comedy writers. But many double-edged remarks are purely accidental, and can occur anywhere. Newspaper headlines are often unintentionally funny, like the following:

SHELL FOUND ON BEACH

PHONES DEAD AFTER FATAL CRASH

INJURY FORCES TENNIS STAR TO SCRATCH

SUPER TRAIN TALKS

Up to scratch ...

DOUBLE MEANING

You don't say!

Besides double meanings, there are other pitfalls for the unwary writer or speaker. Words have a habit of tripping you up, if you are not careful, like the reporter who wrote: 'He has waited 26 years to meet the brother he never knew he had.'

The encyclopedia writer who described lifeboats as 'boats that are specially designed to stay afloat' was not wrong — but, of course, no boat is designed to sink! Here are some more examples of stating what is obvious:

Parents' crucial role in family life is stressed. (Book review)

This match was settled either side of half time. (Football commentator)

If you've got a birthday coming up in the next twelve months or so, ring in ... (Radio phone-in)

Gwent is a county in south-east Wales. The county is strongly Welsh in character. The majority of the people are of Welsh stock and consider themselves to be Welsh. (Encyclopedia entry)

School board agrees to discuss education. (Newspaper headline)

Couple found slain: Police suspect homicide. (Newspaper headline)

If the strike isn't settled quickly, it may last a while. (Radio report)

These medicines might cause drowsiness. (Warning on bottle of sleeping pills)

Which side?

A writer describing the effects of nerve gas was not guilty of *double meaning* or of stating the obvious, but the end result was just as embarrassing: 'Severe exposure causes drowsiness, depression, difficulty in speaking, convulsions and finally death. The effects may last for weeks.'
You don't say!

That was a close one!

'His quick thinking saved an RAF jet pilot from a near disaster'!

(*Newspaper report*)

CONFUSABLES

3 A mute point

Some people confuse words that have a similar sound. An example is 'moot', which means to 'put forward for consideration', and 'mute', which means 'to silence'. A sporting item read: 'The manager has been sacked and former bosses Bobby Gould and Dave Bassett have been muted for the job.'

Fewer or less?

There are hundreds of these 'confusables' in English, and not all are connected with the sounds of the words. 'Less' and 'fewer' and 'can' and 'may' often cause confusion.

The generally accepted 'rule' is that 'fewer' is used with numbers: 'I take fewer lumps of sugar in my coffee than you.' 'Less' applies to quantity: 'I take less sugar in my coffee than you.' It's as simple as that!

Can or may?

The difference between 'can' and 'may' is not quite so clear cut. A general rule is to remember that 'can'
(continued on page 12)

Pouring over a newspaper

Muted managers

See if you can tell the difference in meaning between these 'look-alikes' (answers on page 27):

1 adverse / averse
2 beach / beech
3 callous / callus
4 dual / duel
5 entomology / etymology
6 heroin / heroine
7 kerb / curb
8 lava / larva
9 mantel / mantle
10 naval / navel
11 sew / sow
12 wreath / wreathe

CONFUSABLES

Suspect words

Using your dictionary, see if you can replace any wrong words in these sentences. If you think the word is correct, can you say which word it is usually confused with? The 'suspect' words are printed in heavy black type. (answers are on page 28)

1. She worked in the **personal** office.
2. The trio **includes** a piano, a double bass and a clarinet.
3. His cold **effected** his singing.
4. A whirlwind **raised** the house to the ground.
5. The head is a **stickler** for discipline.
6. The dentist **ensured** me it would not hurt.
7. The firefighter was **hailed** as a hero.
8. The French students are taking their **aural** examinations.
9. They are building an office block on the empty **sight** next to the station.
10. Isaac Newton was a famous **astrologer**.
11. Would you like to **bathe** in the sea?
12. She **poured** over the morning paper, while her husband buttered his toast.
13. The appeal court **squashed** the conviction for armed robbery.
14. It is difficult to **breath** in the thin air up here.
15. The music played in the shop is **oriented** towards young people.
16. The producer **complimented** her on her performance.
17. We sat down to a **luxuriant** banquet.
18. He is most **punctual** in performing every detail.
19. The value of the dollar has **deprecated** since 1991.
20. He **prized** the window open with a large screwdriver.

Would you like a bath?

CONFUSABLES

(continued from page 10)
refers to abililty or opportunity to do something, while 'may' suggests a possibility or permission: 'Tess can play the trombone and may play in the school concert.' But it could be thought over fussy to try to make any distinction between 'Can I come with you?' and 'May I come with you?'

Imply or infer?
'Imply' and 'infer' are words that are often mistakenly used in place of each other. 'Infer' means to draw a conclusion; 'imply' means to suggest something without saying so directly: 'I am forced to infer from that statement that you are implying that I'm a liar!' A speaker implies, a listener infers. However, many great writers — Milton and Jane Austen, for instance — make no distinction.

One or more
We probably all know that the singular is used when there is one person or thing doing something: 'This ball bounces high.' The plural is for more than one: 'These balls bounce high.' Which all seems easy enough. But some words and expressions can cause confusion. For example, is 'none' singular or plural? The answer is that it depends on what it refers to. If it has the meaning not one it is singular: 'None of my sisters looks like my mother.' If it means not any, it may be plural: 'None of the runners have reached the half-way mark.' In this case the singular would also be acceptable. And when 'none' refers to amount, it is also singular: 'None of the salad was eaten.' All clear?

'Collective nouns', or collectives, can be quite tricky. They are sometimes treated as singular and sometimes as plural. Collectives such as 'luggage' or 'equipment' are singular. Those such as 'people' or 'police' are always plural. So you refer to luggage as 'it' and to people or the police as 'they' or 'them'. But

*Who **is** or **are** famous?*

CONFUSABLES

collectives such as 'audience' and 'committee' may be either singular or plural. You might say 'the audience is very quiet tonight,' but you would have to say 'the audience are now taking their seats'. It would sound very odd to say 'the audience is taking its seat' or 'the audience is taking their seats'.

Sports teams also seem to give trouble in this matter. Do you say 'AC Milan is top of the Italian League' or 'AC Milan are .....?' Is it 'Brazil are the best South American team' or 'Brazil is....?' The answer is that both are correct.

But if you have used the singular '*is*', you must also use 'it' — so you might find yourself writing: 'Brazil is the best South American team. It has played in the finals tournament of every World Cup.' That doesn't sound quite right does it? Yet in American English the singular is preferred: 'The LA Lakers is the best basketball team. It has a reputation for exciting play.' It is curious that in the United States, where most teams are referred to by their plural nicknames — the New York Yankees, the Miami Dolphins — the singular should be common usage, whereas the plural is mostly used in Britain. So although the Yankees *is* a famous American football team, Celtic *are* a famous Scottish football club.

One or more

See if you can correct the following sentences where necessary (answers on page 29):

1. Some folk is never satisfied.
2. Although they appeared to agree at first, the committee has broken up in disorder.
3. Everyone is welcome.
4. Anyone can play, can't they?
5. Twenty kilometres is too far for me to walk in an afternoon.
6. One of the planes are missing.
7. A number of tourists arrives every year.
8. The greater part of the apple was mouldy.
9. The greater part of the apples was mouldy.
10. All that's left are some mouldy apples.

A rotten apple

MISTRANSLATIONS

4 I am a jam doughnut

In 1963, the President of the United States, John F. Kennedy, made a speech in Berlin, Germany. He finished with his famous phrase in German: 'Ich bin ein Berliner.' What he had meant to say was: 'I am a Berliner.' What he actually said was: 'I am a jam doughnut.'

Mistakes like the President made frequently happen in translation where the person making the translation is not familiar with all the special expressions of another language. The article 'a' is 'ein' in German. But 'ein' is not used in front of nationalities or other words for people belonging to a particular place. So the president should have said 'Ich bin Berliner'. It was unlucky for him that a Berliner also means a special kind of jam doughnut for which Berlin is famous!

Translating troubles

English-speaking people travelling abroad are often surprised how well people whose first language is not English speak it. Nevertheless some of the biggest howlers appear on notices and instructions for tourists. A souvenir shop in Majorca gave the game away before a word was spoken: 'English well talking. Here speeching American.'

This notice appeared in a tailor's shop on another Mediterranean island, Rhodes: 'Order your summer suit here. Because is big rush, we will execute our customers in strict rotation.' Of course, you execute orders — but not, one would imagine, customers!

Here is a quaint translation from a Japanese car rental company with advice on how and when to use the horn: 'When a passenger of foot heave in sight, tootle the horn. Trumpet him melodiously at first, but if he still obstacles your passage then tootle him with vigour.'

MISTRANSLATIONS

Here are some more howlers from signs and notices in non-English-speaking countries:

1 Gentlemen's throats cut with nice sharp razors (Notice in a Zanzibar barbers)
2 Teeth extracted by the latest Methodists (A Hong Kong dentist)
3 We take your bags and send them in all directions (Copenhagen airline ticket)
4 The lift is being fixed. During that time we regret that you will be unbearable (Sign in a Bucharest hotel)

5 Dropping bricks

GAFFES

The expression 'to drop a brick' means to do or say something terribly embarrassing, usually without realizing it at first. Such gaffes are often made at parties when you try to make conversation with people you only half know — like the man who, on being introduced to a women, asked her: 'What happened to the blonde bimbo your husband used to be married to?' After a cold pause came the reply: 'I dyed my hair.'

The Plain English Campaign is an organization that promotes the use of simple English and fights to stamp out the 'gobbledygook' and jargon found in so many contracts and legal documents. But the organization has itself been caught out. In a brochure advertising an international conference of the campaign appears this sentence: 'One of the keys to plain English is to avoid passive verbs. Unlike American children,

GAFFES

most pupils in UK schools are never taught the difference between the active and passive voice.'

There is nothing wrong grammatically with this extract. But if you are going to recommend avoiding passive verbs, it is not too clever to use one in the very next sentence. (And for the benefit of the poor deprived British childen referred to in the brochure, 'They **gave** me a present' uses an active verb, while 'I **was given** a present' uses a passive verb.)

> **See if you can turn these passive sentences into active ones (answers on page 30):**
> 1 Sam was sold an ice cream by Jack.
> 2 The match between Brazil and Korea was postponed by the management.
> 3 A mouse was caught by our cat.
> 4 The whole house was decorated by the painters last week.
> 5 The play was written by Oscar Wilde.
>
> **Transitive and Intransitive**
> A transitive verb needs a direct object to complete the sense: Jim *likes* chocolates — you can't just *like*.
> An intransitive verb denotes an action that is not performed upon an object — Sara *walked* for miles.

Insults

Dropped bricks are accidental, and may cause offence. Insults, however, are deliberate, and are meant to cause offence. The pen, indeed, is mightier than the sword.

> That's the point of quotations, you know; you can use another's words to be insulting.
> 'Amanda Cross'

Lady Astor to Winston Churchill: Winston, if I were married to you, I'd put poison in your coffee.
Churchill: Nancy, if you were my wife, I'd drink it.

MP Bessie Braddock to Winston Churchill: 'Winston, you're drunk.'
Churchill: 'Bessie, you're ugly, but tomorrow I'll be sober.'

On King Charles II:
Here lies a great and mighty king,
Whose promises none relies on;
He never said a foolish thing,
Nor ever did a wise one.

GAFFES

The actress Bette Davis:
The best time I ever had with Joan Crawford was when I pushed her down the stairs in *Whatever Happened to Baby Jane?*

Composer Gioacchino Rossini:
Wagner has beautiful moments, but awful quarter hours.

Alan Bennett on Arianna Stassinopoulos:
So boring, you fall asleep halfway through her name.

On silent actress Norma Shearer:
A face unclouded by thought.

Writer Dorothy Parker on actress Katherine Hepburn:
She ran the whole gamut of the emotions from A to B.

William Faulkner on Ernest Hemingway:
He has never used a word that might send the reader to the dictionary.

Ernest Hemingway on William Faulkner:
Poor Faulkner. Does he really think big emotions come from big words?

Anon referring to Queen Elizabeth I:
Oh dearest Queen
I've never seen
A face more like
A soup-tureen.

Groucho Marx to hostess: I've had a wonderful evening — but this wasn't it.

American composer Aaron Copland:
Listening to the Fifth Symphony of Ralph Vaughan Williams is like staring at a cow for forty-five minutes.

English satirist Samuel Butler:
It was good of God to let Carlyle and Mrs Carlyle marry one another and so make two people miserable instead of four.

The playwright Noel Coward:
Dear Randolph (Churchill) utterly unspoiled by his great failure.

Pauline Kall reviewing 'Dances with Wolves':
[Kevin] Costner has feathers in his hair and feathers in his head.

SOLECISMS

6 It'll be all wrong on the night

English is an ever-changing language. New words and phrases are always appearing. Old ones die out. Some words are misused or misspelt so much that in the end the 'wrong' version becomes accepted. An example of this is the spelling of all right as 'alright'. It used to be all wrong, but now it's pretty much alright!

According to *Chambers Dictionary*, there was no such word as 'alright' until the 1959 edition included it as an 'unacceptable spelling'. But more and more people were writing 'alright' in the belief that this was the correct spelling.

A popular TV show featuring fluffs, howlers and funny visual mistakes on television was called 'It'll be alright on the night', so more people thought it was correct. In 1983 Chambers upgraded 'alright' to 'an alternative, less acceptable spelling', and ten years later added 'much used in informal contexts'.

You can't halt progress
Some teachers and other 'keepers' of the language may continue to fight against what they see as the wrong version of a word. Others might see the wisdom of accepting something that makes sense and does not damage the language. 'Alright' comes into this acceptable category.

Words such as 'altogether', 'always' and 'already' were, after all, originally two words — all together, all ways, and all ready. As often happens in English, two words that are frequently used together to

An all out fight...

convey a single idea or to represent a single thing become one word, sometimes with a hyphen or with the omission of a letter. 'Spoonful', for example, began as 'spoon full', as, in a similar way, did 'hurtful' and all the other 'fuls'. 'Gatepost' began as gate post, 'lipstick' as lip stick, and so on.

To go back to 'alright', some commentators have argued that it would be no bad thing to distinguish

SOLECISMS

between 'alright' and 'all right' as we do between 'already' and 'all ready'. We can see the distinction in a sentence like: 'The spellings are all right, alright?' Here the first meaning is 'all correct', the second meaning is 'OK'.

Look in *Chambers Dictionary* under 'sea' and notice that some compound words are hyphenated, some are still separate words and others have blended into single words:

sea anemone   sea blue
seaboard   seafarer
seafood   seagull
seahorse   sea level
sea lion   seashell
sea-gooseberry   seasick
sea urchin   seaweed

Look up words under 'air' and 'water' and you'll find that similar things happen to them:
air-brush air-conditioner
aircraft air freight air-rifle
waterfall water ice water-heater

Try not to use 'and' with 'try'

You don't have to be a purist to believe that some things are so ugly or so wrong that every effort should be made to resist them. One of these is the expression 'try and' as in:

1 Try and behave yourselves for a change.
2 They always try and stop us enjoying ourselves.
3 Try and make a cake.
4 I shall try and make a good job of it.
5 We expect the children to try and enjoy themselves at the pantomime.

The correct expression is 'try to'. It means the same as 'attempt to' — and you would never say 'attempt and'. Nor would you be able to say 'try and' if you used a negative or a different tense of the verb. Compare the following sentences with 1 to 5 above:

1 Try not to misbehave yourself.
2 They tried to stop us.
3 Are you trying to make a cake?

You wouldn't say 'Try not and misbehave yourself', 'They tried and stop us' or 'Are you trying and make a cake?'

Listen to people speaking on the radio or TV and record how many

I'm trying to make a cake.

SOLECISMS

say 'try and' and how many use the correct 'try to'. Perhaps people find it difficult to say 'try to', and 'try and' trips off the tongue more easily.

Dictionaries and grammar books say 'try and' is used informally. But one of the few instances where it has become an idiom, or saying, is in the warning 'Try and stop me'.

Being literal

Sometimes words that convey a particular meaning are so misused that they are in danger of losing that meaning. An example of this is 'literally', which means 'to the letter', or 'exactly in the way stated, without any exaggeration'. But many people use the word to give emphasis, as in: 'It was literally raining cats and dogs.' They did not mean to say that real cats and dogs were falling from the sky. 'Literally' should never be used in this way. But in this sentence 'literally' is used for an exact description of what happened: 'The wind was so strong that I literally had to crawl the last few metres on my hands and knees.'

Literally raining...

Most unusual — unique

Another word that suffers from misuse is 'unique', which means the only one of a particular kind. Something is either 'unique' or it isn't. It cannot be 'very unique' or 'rather unique'.

What's a solecism?

A solecism is a misuse of what is considered the correct use of the language. Such blunders include most of the mistakes pointed out in this book.

SOLECISMS

Try to suggest a better way of getting the following points across if you think that 'unique' has been misused (answers on page 30):

1 This washing powder is the most unique on the market.
2 The language of the Hocha tribe is more unique than that of their neighbours, the Docha.
3 Their feat of winning fifteen consecutive games is almost unique in the Premier division.
4 That's a rather unique design for a tablecloth .

Ever hopefully

'Hopefully' in the sense of 'let us hope' or 'it is to be hoped' is often used at the beginning of a sentence: 'Hopefully, it has stopped raining.' This usage has long caused purists to get very hot under the collar. They would like to restrict its use to the adverb 'in a hopeful way' as in: 'He spoke hopefully of her full recovery from the fall.' But 'hopefully' in the first 'let us hope' sense is now so widespread that it may (hopefully?) qualify as Standard English. The same probably goes for that much overworked word 'basically' which some people seem to begin every other sentence with. They basically like using the word. Basically, what do you think?

Spot the mistakes. **Can you tell good from bad English? See if you can spot the errors or the unnecessary words in the following (answers on page 30):**

1 You naughty girl, you didn't ought to do that.
2 Was you busy last night?
3 The dog is eating it's bone.
4 That is the widow of the late Mr Smith.
5 Is this book your's or their's?
6 Rabbits eat both the grass, the corn, and the flowers in the field.
7 He don't love me no more.
8 Im not listening to no more of your lies.

(continued on next page)

SOLECISMS

(continued from page 21)

9 She drunk a whole bottle of lemonade.
10 The stadia is full of fans.
11 The cacti needs watering.
12 She sings good but her sister sings best.
13 You could of warned me about that fierce dog.
14 Hyphens break up words as in leg-end, and hear-tily.
15 When he broke his leg he was in intensive pain.
16 Lie the baby on the bed.
17 My bad foot is a bit of a headache, but I can still walk.
18 My cousin and myself were invited to a party.
19 There was no ice cream left, and no lemonade neither.
20 Into the room walks our teacher and her husband.
21 I prefer the flavour of this ice cream the most.
22 They're rather fools.
23 The son of the singer's is learning to play the guitar.
24 What are her future prospects?
25 Our grateful thanks to all who came to the meeting.

My bad foot is a bit of a headache

Twisted words

The United States is the second largest consumer of champagne after the United Kingdom; not so! In fact, the United States is the largest consumer of champagne after the United Kingdom, and the second largest consumer in the world.

NEW WORDS

7 If you can't beat 'em...

Some idioms or expressions creep into English by mistake. For years, the dictionaries and grammar books treat them as blunders, then perhaps as 'informal' expressions. But if more and more people use the 'wrong' version, it becomes difficult to stick to your guns and use what you know to be the right version. In the end, it might be a case of: 'If you can't beat 'em, join 'em.'

A common snack in many parts of Britain is a dish called Welsh rarebit. Most people know what it is — melted cheese (sometimes with ale) on toast. But this used to be known as Welsh rabbit. Then someone, somewhere called it Welsh rare-bit for a joke. The joke caught on, and the 'rarebit' version stuck. Several years later, with 'rarebit' appearing on menus everywhere, even the dictionaries caved in and gave 'Welsh rarebit' pride of place.

A degree in finger-painting

Words sometimes get hijacked. A word may be used in an unusual or particular way, which suddenly becomes trendy. Sooner or later, the new meaning becomes the most used meaning. An example of this is the word 'decimate'.

Like 'decimal', this comes from a Latin word meaning a tenth part. At one time when the ancient Romans went to war, they executed one in every ten of their worst soldiers — the cowardly, mutinous or just not very good ones. This practice of 'decimating' the worst made sure that the others pulled their socks up and gave of their best without questioning their orders.

But the word has come to be used loosely to mean 'to kill or destroy a great part of', usually of the enemy or perhaps innocent bystanders, or 'to reduce heavily'.

In a book called *New Words for Old*, the author Philip Howard describes how the term 'student', once meaning someone studying at university or taking any course of higher education, has been widened, first in

A rare Welsh rabbit ...

America and later in Britain, to cover anyone enrolled in a class, including high school and primary school 'students'. He wondered whether the latter would be taking their degrees in Plasticine and finger painting!

Do you think that there should be a limit to what we should accept in English? What about 'would of' for 'would have' or 'I done it' for 'I did it'? Just because many people use these 'wrong' expressions, is that a good enough reason to accept them?

AMBIGUITY

8 Head-scratching time

A cricket team touring India found themselves up against the Maharashtra Small Savings Minister's XI. It probably didn't bother the players, but does Maharashtra, a state in western India, have a minister for Small Savings, or does it have more than one Savings minister — one of whom happens to be small?

Adding a little dash

When a statement has two possible meanings, we say it is 'ambiguous'. Quite often ambiguity can be avoided by the use of a hyphen. For example, if the cricket team above had been called the Maharashtra Small-Savings Minister's XI, there would not have been any silly jokes about small ministers.

Savings Ministers — large and small

Try placing a hyphen in the following sentences to avoid ambiguity (answers on page 31):

1 There are twenty odd pupils in the class.
2 I enjoy a hard boiled egg for my breakfast.
3 He is the highest rated climber in the world.
4 He is an ill mannered youth.
5 She has nine inch long feet.
6 The king's little used palace is for sale.
7 The long absent dachshund is safely back home.
8 Man eating tiger.
9 A French geography student.
10 A Danish pastry maker.

What is the difference between Geronimo, one of the great North American Indian leaders, and General Custer, who faced the Indians at the Battle of the Alamo? The answer is a hyphen! Geronimo was an Indian fighter, while Custer was an Indian-fighter.

AMBIGUITY

More ambiguity

It is not just a missing hyphen that causes ambiguity. Can you say what is ambiguous about the following sentences? (answers on page 31)

1 Water is available below the surface of the ground, and most of the country's crops are grown there.
2 The German philosopher Nietzsche attracted little attention before he became insane, but later influenced many poets and philosophers.
3 Scientists think that certain swimming muscles in the eel's ancestors changed into electric organs.
4 The British troops came close enough to Port Stanley to see Argentinians eating their dinner through binoculars.
5 Spotted man wanted for questioning (*Newspaper headline*)
6 Icelandic fish talks
7 Erected to the Memory of John McFarlane
   Drown'd in the Water of Leith
   By a few affectionate friends
   (*Inscription on Edinburgh tombstone*)

Well spotted ...

TIME CONFUSION

9 Hi there! What's the time?

The time is five minutes past midnight. As the radio presenter opens her phone-in programme after the 12 o'clock news, it is dark outside and dawn is a long way off. What does she say to her listeners, most of whom have not yet gone to bed? She says 'Good morning'. Not by any stretch of the imagination is it morning, yet people think that because the time is 12.05 a.m. they have to say 'Good morning'.

The letters a.m. and p.m. stand for Latin words, *ante meridiem* (before noon) and *post meridiem* (after noon), which are used to divide a day into two 12-hour periods. The abbreviation a.m., does not mean 'morning' — it simply refers to the 12 hours before noon, just as p.m. refers to the 12 hours after noon. So the greetings 'Good morning' and 'Good afternoon' are not really connected with these abbreviations. After all, you would not say 'Good afternoon' at 8 p.m. You would say 'Good evening' or, if you were going to bed or leaving someone, 'Good night'.

We could all adopt the Australian habit of saying 'Good day' (G'day) which they use at any time of day. What do you think? Or maybe you like the traditional British variations: Good morning, Good afternoon, Good evening and Good night. But there again, perhaps many of you simply say 'Hi!'.

ANSWERS

1 Between you and me and the gatepost
The right pronouns (page 5)
1 *The prize was given jointly to **him** and his sister.*
2 *This is from my brother and **me**.*
3 *My mother and **I** enjoy a game of Scrabble.*
4 *The argument is between **them** and **us**.*
5 ***He** and **she** are identical twins.*
6 *It was **I** who broke the cup.*
7 *Who's that at the door. It's **me**. (By itself, without a following 'who' clause, 'me' is accepted English. In fact, 'It's I' or 'It is I' is never used.)*
8 *You and **I** make a good partnership.*

Self sacrifice (page 6)
1 *Put yourself in my place.(OK)*
2 *I'm going to choose the books myself. (OK — 'myself' here is used for emphasis.)*
3 *They found themselves in an awkward situation. (OK)*
4 *No one has informed either **me** or my parents.*
5 *She left it for Peter and **me**.*
6 *Jack, the twins and **I** were the only ones present.*
7 *How are **you**?*
8 *I built the house myself. (OK)*
9 *The kittens were presents for my brother and **me**.*
10 *The teacher gave **us** a lesson.*

A suitable case for treatment (page 7)
Is that Jane Smith? — 'This is Jane Smith', or 'Jane Smith speaking' or simply 'Speaking' are all acceptable.

3 A mute point
Look-alikes (page 10)
1 ***Adverse** means unfavourable: 'adverse weather'; **averse** means opposed to: 'I'm not averse to helping you'.*
2 ***Beach** is the sea shore; **beech** is a type of tree.*
3 ***Callous** means lacking any concern for others; **callus** an area of hard skin.*
4 ***Dual** means having two parts (dual personality); **duel** is a fight between two people.*
5 ***Entomology** is the study of insects; **etymology** is the study of the meaning of words.*
6 ***Heroin** is a habit-forming

drug; **heroine** is a woman admired for her courage.

7 **Kerb** stones form the edge of a pavement; **curb** is to restrain.

8 **Lava** is molten rock flowing from a volcano; **larva** a developing insect, e.g. a caterpillar.

9 **Mantel** is the ornamental frame around a fireplace — mantelpiece; **mantle** a cloak.

10 **Naval** means concerning the navy; **navel** a hollow in the belly.

11 **Sew** is to stitch; **sow** is to plant seeds.

12 **Wreath** is a ring-shaped garland of flowers; **wreathe** means to coil or intertwine.

Suspect words (page 11)

1 She worked in the **personnel** office. (**Personal** is 'private' or 'relating to a person'; **personnel** means 'staff'.)

2 The trio **comprises** or **consists of** a piano, double bass and clarinet. (**Include** implies a selection, but there are only three instruments or players in a trio.)

3 His cold **affected** his singing. (This use of **affect** means to 'have an **effect** on'.)

4 A whirlwind **razed** the house to the ground. (**Raze**, usually applied to buildings, means to level or to tear down completely; **raise** is to lift up.)

5 The head is a **stickler** for discipline. (Correct. A person who insists on something; often confused with **sticker**, someone who perseveres or 'sticks at' a task.)

6 The dentist **assured** me it would not hurt. (You **assure** a person of something; to **ensure** is to make certain of something; and to **insure** is guarantee against loss, by taking out insurance.)

7 The firefighter was **hailed** as a hero. (Correct. **Hail** means to greet or acclaim, and also to bombard with things such as missiles or abuse; **hale** means to drag, as in front of a judge. It also means healthy.)

8 The French students are taking their **oral** examinations. (**Oral** relates to the mouth, so an 'oral exam' is a spoken one; **aural** refers to the ear.)

9 They are building an office block on the empty **site** next to the station. (A **site** is a piece of land; a **sight**, among other things, something worth seeing.)

10 Isaac Newton was a famous **astronomer**. (**Astronomers** are people who make a

scientific study of the stars and planets; **astrologers** mostly try to predict people's future from their birth date and the movement of the heavenly bodies.)

11 Would you like to **bathe** in the sea? (Correct. **Bathe** is to swim or bask, and may also mean to wash or moisten something, such as a wound. To **bath**, the word it is sometimes confused with, is what you do in a bath, wash yourself.)

12 She **pored** over the morning paper while her husband buttered his toast. (**Pore** over means to study closely; **pour** is something you do with liquid such as tea.)

13 The appeal court **quashed** the conviction for armed robbery. (To **quash** is to abolish.)

14 It is difficult to **breathe** in the thin air up here. (**Breathe** is what you do when you take in air and expel it; **breath** is the air breathed).

15 The music played in the shop is **oriented** towards young people. (Correct, and so is **orientated**, which means exactly the same. However, they are overused words, and often, as here, **directed** would be better.)

16 The producer **complimented** her on her performance. (Correct. **Compliment** means 'to praise'; **complement** means to 'fill out' or 'to make whole'.)

17 We sat down to a **luxurious** banquet. (**Luxurious** means sumptuous and expensive; **luxuriant** means 'profuse growth'.)

18 He is most **punctilious** in performing every detail. (**Punctilious** means 'careful, attentive'; **punctual** means 'on time'.)

19 The value of the dollar has **depreciated** since 1991. (**Depreciated** means 'to fall in value'; **deprecate** means 'to express disapproval of'.)

20 He **prised** the window open with a large screwdriver. (**Prise** is to force with a lever; **prize** is to value highly.)

One or more (page 13)

1 Some folk **are** never satisfied. ('Folk', like 'people', is plural.)

2 Although they appeared to agree at first, the committee **have** broken up in disorder. ('Committee' is referred to as **they**, so you must use the plural of the verb.)

3 Everyone **is** welcome. (Correct)

4 Anyone can play, can't **they**?

(This is OK. Anyone is normally singular, but to say 'can't he?' or 'can't she' would sound odd.)
  5 *Twenty kilometres **is** too far for me to walk in an afternoon. (Correct. This is a distance, not a number of separate kilometres.)*
  6 *One of the planes **is** missing.*
  7 *A number of tourists **arrive** every year. (It's not the 'number' that arrives but the 'tourists'.)*
  8 *The greater part of the apple **was** mouldy. (Correct. 'Greater part' refers to quantity.)*
  9 *The greater part of the apples **were** mouldy. (Here, 'greater part' refers to a number, say 8 of 12 apples, being mouldy.)*
  10 *All that's left **is** some mouldy apples. (You use the singular to agree with 'that's' — that is. But it is also correct to say: 'All that are left are some mouldy apples.')*

5 Dropping bricks
Passive into active
(page 16)
  1 *Jack sold Sam an ice cream.*
  2 *The management postponed the match between Brazil and Korea.*
  3 *Our cat caught a mouse.*
  4 *The painters decorated the whole house last week.*
  5 *Oscar Wilde wrote the play.*

6 It'll be all wrong. . .
Unique (page 21)
The following are just examples of acceptable sentences:
  1 *This washing powder has unique properties.*
  2 *The language of the Hocha tribe is spoken by fewer people than that of their neighbours, the Docha.*
  3 *Their feat of winning fifteen consecutive games is almost unique in the Premier Division. (This is OK — 'almost unique' implies that it has been done before, perhaps once or twice.)*
  4 *That's an unusual design for a tablecloth.*

Spot the mistakes
(pages 21–22)
  1 *You naughty girl, you **shouldn't** do that.*
  2 ***Were** you busy last night?*
  3 *The dog is eating **its** bone.*
  4 *That is the widow of Mr Smith. (If he has a widow, he must be dead, and therefore 'late'.)*
  5 *Is this book **yours** or **theirs**.*
  6 *Rabbits eat the grass, the corn and the flowers in the field. (**Both** refer to only two things.)*

7 He **doesn't** love me **any** more.
8 **I'm** not listening to **any** more of your lies.
9 She **drank** a whole bottle of lemonade.
10 The stadia **are** full of fans. (Stadium is singular.)
11 The cacti **need** watering (Cactus is the singular.)
12 She sings **well** but her sister sings **better**.
13 You could **have** warned me about that fierce dog.
14 Hyphens break up words, as in **le**-gend and **heart**-ily.
15 When he broke his leg he was in **intense** pain.
16 **Lay** the baby on the bed.
17 My bad foot is a bit of a **nuisance** (or some word other than headache).
18 My cousin and **I** were invited to a party.
19 There was no ice cream left, and no lemonade **either**.
20 Into the room **walk** our teacher and her husband.
21 I **like** the flavour of this ice cream the most.
22 They're rather **foolish**.
23 The **singer's** son is learning to play the guitar.
24 What are her prospects? (Prospects are 'future'.)
25 Our thanks to all who came to the meeting. (Grateful is unnecessary.)

8 Head-scratching time
Hyphenating (page 24)
1 There are **twenty-odd** pupils in the class.
2 I enjoy a **hard-boiled** egg for my breakfast.
3 He is the **highest-rated** climber in the world.
4 He is an **ill-mannered** youth.
5 She has **nine-inch-long** feet.
6 The king's **little-used** palace is for sale.
7 The **long-absent** dachshund is safely back home.
8 **Man-eating** tiger.
9 A **French-geography** student or A French **geography-student**.
10 A **Danish-pastry** maker or A Danish **pastry-maker**.

More ambiguity (page 25)
1 It appears as if most of the country's crops are grown underground.
2 It was the works of Nietzsche that influenced others after he became insane.

3 *'Electric organs', best known as very large musical instruments, is an unfortunate expression here for body organs with electrical properties.*
4 *Words ('through binoculars') in the wrong place make a nonsense of the sentence.*
5 *A man wanted for questioning was seen (spotted).*
6 *The fish didn't talk — there were talks about the Icelandic fish dispute.*
7 *This seems as if his friends drowned him.*

Standard English is the speech or 'dialect' of the upper and upper-middle classes. It is normally used in writing English and teaching it to foreigners.

RP — Received Pronunciation — is the pronunciation of that variety of English widely considered to be least regional, being originally that used by the educated people in southern England. RP is a neutral, national standard.